Red Gerard

by Grace Hansen

OLYMPIC BIOGRAPHIES

Abdo Kids Jumbo is an Imprint of Abdo Kids
abdopublishing.com

abdopublishing.com

Published by Abdo Kids, a division of ABDO, P.O. Box 398166, Minneapolis, Minnesota 55439.
Copyright © 2019 by Abdo Consulting Group, Inc. International copyrights reserved in all countries.
No part of this book may be reproduced in any form without written permission from the publisher.
Abdo Kids Jumbo™ is a trademark and logo of Abdo Kids.

052018

092018

Photo Credits: AP Images, Getty Images, iStock, Shutterstock

Production Contributors: Teddy Borth, Jennie Forsberg, Grace Hansen

Design Contributors: Dorothy Toth, Laura Mitchell

Library of Congress Control Number: 2018936105

Publisher's Cataloging in Publication Data

Names: Hansen, Grace, author.

Title: Red Gerard / by Grace Hansen.

Description: Minneapolis, Minnesota : Abdo Kids, 2019 | Series: Olympic
    biographies set 2 | Includes glossary, index and online resources (page 24).

Identifiers: ISBN 9781532181450 (lib. bdg.) | ISBN 9781532181559 (ebook) |
    ISBN 9781532181603 (Read-to-me ebook)

Subjects: LCSH: Olympic athletes--Juvenile literature. | Winter Olympics--
    Juvenile literature. | Snowboarders--Juvenile literature.

Classification: DDC 796.93092 [B]--dc23

Table of Contents

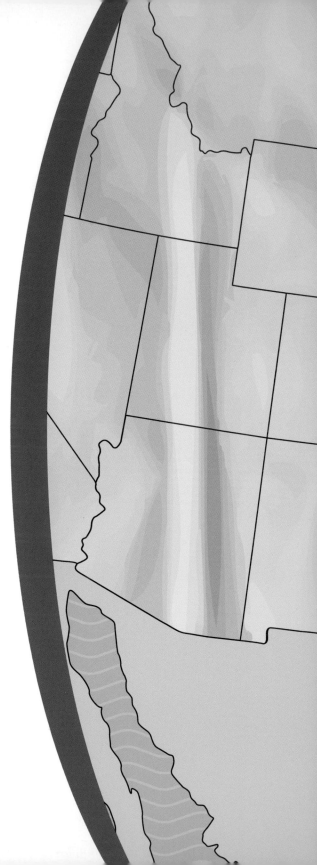

Early Years

Redmond Gerard was born on June 29, 2000, in Westlake, Ohio. He is the sixth of seven children. He began snowboarding when he was 2 years old.

Westlake

By the time Red was 6, his family knew he had a gift. The Gerards moved to Colorado in 2007. Living near the mountains was great for Red.

Going Pro

Red made his **pro debut** at the 2016 Dew Tour. Soon after, he earned a spot on the US pro team. He was just 15 years old.

8

9

Red's first Winter X Games was in 2017. One year later, he competed at the 2018 US Grand Prix. He needed to be the best American in **slopestyle**. This would get him to the Olympics.

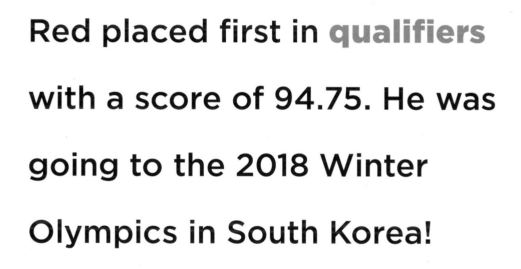

Red placed first in **qualifiers** with a score of 94.75. He was going to the 2018 Winter Olympics in South Korea!

12

13

Red Sees Gold

Red was an **underdog** in South Korea. But he was the only American to make it to the finals in **slopestyle**.

Red's first two runs in the finals were not his best. He received low scores for mistakes.

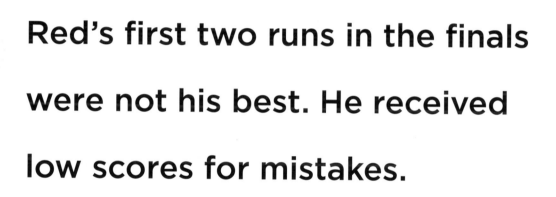

16

On his third run he nailed his first two jumps. He finished with a backside triple cork **1440**. Red describes the move as, "Just a whole bunch of spins."

PyeongChang 2018

Red won the gold with a score of 87.16! The future for this fearless boarder looks bright!

More Facts

- **Slopestyle** boarders are mostly judged on how hard their tricks are, how many tricks they do, and how well they land them.

- Red Gerard is known for his relaxed attitude on the course.

- On the morning of his big run at the Olympics, Red woke up late and lost his jacket. He had to borrow a jacket from his teammate.

Glossary

debut – a person's first appearance in a particular role.

1440 – four full rotations.

pro – short for professional.

qualifier – a match or contest to decide which individuals or teams qualify for a competition.

slopestyle – an event where a snowboarder moves down a course with a variety of obstacles including rails, jumps, and other terrain park features.

underdog – a competitor thought to have little chance of winning a contest.

Index

**Abdo Kids
ONLINE**
FREE! ONLINE MULTIMEDIA RESOURCES

Visit **abdokids.com** and use this code to access crafts, games, videos, and more!

Abdo Kids Code:
ORK1450

24